YOUR KNOWLEDGE HAS VALUE

Stanko Radmilovic

World, Europe, Serbia. A comparative analysis of the most important relationships and interactions

GRIN Verlag

Bibliografische Information der Deutschen Nationalbibliothek:

Die Deutsche Bibliothek verzeichnet diese Publikation in der Deutschen National-
bibliografie; detaillierte bibliografische Daten sind im Internet über http://dnb.d-
nb.de/ abrufbar.

Imprint:

Copyright © 2013 GRIN Verlag GmbH
Druck und Bindung: Books on Demand GmbH, Norderstedt Germany
ISBN: 978-3-656-59244-0

This book at GRIN:

http://www.grin.com/en/e-book/267111/world-europe-serbia-a-comparative-analysis-
of-the-most-important-relationships

GRIN - Your knowledge has value

Der GRIN Verlag publiziert seit 1998 wissenschaftliche Arbeiten von Studenten, Hochschullehrern und anderen Akademikern als eBook und gedrucktes Buch. Die Verlagswebsite www.grin.com ist die ideale Plattform zur Veröffentlichung von Hausarbeiten, Abschlussarbeiten, wissenschaftlichen Aufsätzen, Dissertationen und Fachbüchern.

World, Europe, Serbia - A comparative analysis of the most important relationships and interactions

Prof. dr Stanko Radmilović

The subject of this comparative analysis of the most important macroeconomic relationships and interactions in a sample of 46 countries, including most developed countries Europe, but the largest non-European countries that are developing rapidly. That give a twofold result. An insight into the changes in the global balance "economic power". The second, better understanding of milieu EU, which Serbia considers as "Port Hope", which will not only receive us with open arms, then would be willing to drag our little boat, which was in poor condition, in the last resort but without a lot of our efforts and sweat.

Comprehensive analysis exists in the Serbian language in the article "Europe in the world, Serbia in Europe - Comparative Analysis of the most important relationships and interactions." There, in English, are specified section titles, and at the end the Integral table with integral numerical factography

1. The level of GDP per capita and GDP growth rates, show major and divergent imbalances in the modern, globalized world economy

2. The necessity of distinguishing and applying appropriate statement in a constant value in the current (current) value of U.S. $

3. Large differences / imbalances in the achieved level of real GDP per capita and current rates of real economic growth

3.1. Large differences / imbalances in the level of real GDP per capita

3.2. Large differences in rates of economic growth - "counter-imbalance" enormous differences in per capita GDP

4. Even though it does not say so openly and loudly, in the area of commodity markets and aggregate demand are the primary causes of many imbalances - and the global crisis

5. Searching for the causes of uneven economic growth in the number of relationships and interdependencies in the formation and use of GDP

5.1. In most developed countries, there is an evident trend of neglecting the real economy favoring the formatting GDP from services, particularly financial - the phenomenon of financialization

5.2. Government final consumption and final consumption of households have a significant impact on the level of savings, investment and economic growth

5.3. Levels of domestic investment and domestic savings - an important
determinant of economic growth, and foreign debt

6. Just some of the crucial dilemmas of EU integration of Serbia,
which imposed factography and elaboration in this article

Integral factography of GDP per capita as an indicator of the level of development, its growth rate
as indicators of the dynamics of development, the determinants in domain formation and use of
GDP and its implications in the form of external debt per capita

						Arithmetic averages of annual percent after 2000					
Zemlje	GDP per capita (current US$) u 2011	GDP per capita (constant 2000 US$) u 2011	GDP growth (annual %)	Agricult. value added (% of GDP)	Industry, value added (% of GDP)	Services, etc., value added (% of GDP)	Household final consumpt. Expendit., etc. (% of GDP)	General governm. final consumpt. Expendit. (% of GDP)	Gross capital formation (% of GDP)	Gross domestic savings (% of GDP)	External debt stocks(DOD, current US$, per capita), u 2010
1	2	3	4	5	6	7	8	9	10	11	12
Alb.	4.030	1.966	5,4	23,3	19,9	56,8	87,9	9,2	26,3	2,8	1.478
Arg.	10.941	11.602	4,1	8,8	32,4	58,8	62,1	13,1	19,3	24,9	3.164
Astrl.	60.642	25.351	3,1	3,1	24,3	72,6	57,0	17,4	26,8	25,6	52.422
Austri.	49.707	27.428	1,8	1,8	29,6	68,7	54,4	18,7	22,7	26,9	89.991
Belar	5.820	2.890	7,3	10,5	40,9	48,6	56,0	19,3	30,4	24,7	2.711
Belg.	46.469	24.734	1,6	1,0	24,2	74,8	52,2	22,7	21,4	25,1	113.897
B - H	4.821	2.225	4,2	9,5	25,5	65	92,7	21,6	21,9	-16,7	2.249
Braz.	12.594	4.803	3,7	6,0	28,0	66,0	61,0	20,1	17,8	18,9	1.780
Bulg.	7.158	2.618	4,3	9,1	29,1	61,9	67,6	18,0	26,1	14,5	6.381
Can.	50.345	25.933	2,2	1,6	26,1	54,1	56,3	19,7	21,3	24,0	34.607
China	5.430	2.635	10,3	12,2	46,5	41,3	39,2	14,4	41,9	46,4	410
Croat.	14.488	6.352	2,8	5,6	28,0	66,5	58,9	20,8	26,1	20,3	13.513
Czech	20.407	7.912	3,5	0,0	0,0	0,0	50,2	21,0	27,6	28,8	8.250
Denm.	59.684	30.687	0,9	1,7	25,0	73,3	48,0	26,7	20,5	25,3	100.853
Eston.	16.556	6.438	4,3	0,0	0,0	0,0	55,1	18,6	30,4	26,3	15.134
Finl.	49.391	27.766	2,2	3,0	32,4	64,7	51,6	22,3	20,5	26,1	69.136
Fran.	42.377	23.017	1,4	2,4	21,1	76,5	56,9	23,6	19,9	19,5	72.193
Germ.	43.689	26.081	1,2	1,0	29,3	69,6	57,9	19,0	18,6	23,1	57.632
Gre.	26.427	12.653	2,4	0,0	0,0	0,0	70,4	18,4	23,2	11,1	47.095
Hung.	14.044	5.746	2,2	4,4	30,4	65,2	54,7	22,2	23,4	23,0	14.840
India	1.489	838	7,2	19,6	27,3	53,1	59,8	11,4	31,6	28,8	237
Irel.	48.423	27.329	2,5	1,9	36,2	61,9	47,5	16,6	22,2	35,9	27.503
Italy	36.116	18.935	0,7	2,3	26,9	70,8	59,3	19,8	20,9	20,9	36.754
Jap.	45.903	39.578	0,9	1,3	28,4	70,3	57,9	18,4	22,5	23,7	19.153
Korea	22.424	16.684	4,6	3,4	37,3	59,3	54,4	13,9	29,5	31,6	7.490
Latv.	12.726	5.331	4,3	4,0	22,4	73,6	62,6	19,2	29,7	18,2	17.666
Lithu.	13.339	5.793	4,5	4,6	30,9	64,5	65,0	20,1	21,7	14,8	9.006
Macd.	4.925	2.284	2,7	11,9	29,6	58,5	76,4	19,5	22,6	4,0	2.817
Mold.	1.967	635	4,9	18,6	18,0	63,3	91,1	18,2	27,5	-9,2	1.296

Monte.	7.197	2.278	3,7	10,7	21,8	67,5	84,3	19,9	24,0	-4,2	2.462
Nether.	50.087	26.735	1,6	2,2	24,4	73,4	48,1	24,9	19,9	27,0	113.418
Norw.	98.102	40.035	1,7	1,6	40,9	57,6	43,1	20,7	21,5	36,2	131.513
Pol.	13.463	6.854	3,9	4,4	30,8	64,8	63,4	18,1	21,2	18,5	6.623
Portu.	22.330	11.559	0,9	2,9	25,3	71,8	64,6	20,3	23,8	15,1	46.797
Rom.	8.406	2.633	4,2	10,8	33,3	56,0	72,1	11,2	25,1	16,7	5.668
Russ.	13.089	3.052	5,4	5,3	35,8	58,9	49,4	17,6	21,4	32,9	2.711
Serb.	6.203	1.221	3,9	13,2	28,6	58,2	79,7	20,3	20,8	0,0	4.663
Slvak	17.646	8.694	4,5	4,2	36,3	59,5	57,6	19,3	26,5	23,1	10.926
Slven.	24.142	12.689	2,9	2,7	34,1	63,2	55,0	19,0	26,8	26,0	25.173
Spain	32.244	15.512	2,4	3,4	28,6	68,0	57,9	18,4	27,6	23,7	47.014
Swe.	56.927	33.513	2,4	1,8	27,5	70,7	48,2	26,5	18,2	25,3	90.988
Switz.	80.391	38.060	1,9	1,3	27,2	71,5	59,1	11,4	21,3	29,5	153.332
Turk.	10.498	5.741	4,3	10,2	28,5	61,4	70,5	12,7	19,2	16,8	4.039
Ukra.	3.615	1.094	4,7	11,2	34,1	54,7	58,8	19,0	22,1	22,2	2.546
U. K.	38.818	28.033	2,0	0,8	23,8	75,4	64,7	21,0	16,9	14,3	144.316
U. S.	48.442	37.691	1,8	1,2	21,7	77,2	70,2	16,0	18,3	13,9	15.814

Sources and categorical explanatory:

Col. 2: GDP per capita (current US$) - GDP per capita is gross domestic product divided by midyear population. GDP is the sum of gross value added by all resident producers in the economy plus any product taxes and minus any subsidies not included in the value of the products. It is calculated without making deductions for depreciation of fabricated assets or for depletion and degradation of natural resources. Data are in current U.S. dollars. (Izvor: WB WD Indicators, 27.7.2012)

Col. 3: GDP per capita u 2011 (constant 2000 US$) - GDP per capita is gross domestic product divided by midyear population. GDP is the sum of gross value added by all resident producers in the economy plus any product taxes and minus any subsidies not included in the value of the products. It is calculated without making deductions for depreciation of fabricated assets or for depletion and degradation of natural resources. Data are in constant U.S. dollars. (Izvor: WB WD Indicators, 27.7.2012)

Col. 4: GDP per capita growth (annual %) - Annual percentage growth rate of GDP per capita based on constant local currency. GDP per capita is gross domestic product divided by midyear population. GDP at purchaser's prices is the sum of gross value added by all resident producers in the economy plus any product taxes and minus any subsidies not included in the value of the products. It is calculated without making deductions for depreciation of fabricated assets or for depletion and degradation of natural resources. (Izvor: WB WD Indicators, 27.7.2012)

Col. 5: Agriculture, value added (% of GDP) - Agriculture corresponds to ISIC divisions 1-5 and includes forestry, hunting, and fishing, as well as cultivation of crops and livestock production. Value added is the net output of a sector after adding up all outputs and subtracting intermediate inputs. It is calculated without making deductions for depreciation of fabricated assets or depletion and degradation of natural resources. The origin of value added is determined by the International Standard Industrial Classification (ISIC), revision 3. Note: For VAB countries, gross value added at factor cost is used as the denominator. (Izvor: WB WD Indicators, 5.8.212.)

Col. 6: Industry, value added (% of GDP) - Industry corresponds to ISIC divisions 10-45 and includes manufacturing (ISIC divisions 15-37). It comprises value added in mining, manufacturing (also reported as a separate subgroup), construction, electricity, water, and gas. Value added is the net output of a sector after adding up all outputs and subtracting intermediate inputs. It is calculated without making deductions for depreciation of fabricated assets or depletion and degradation of natural resources. The origin of value added is determined by the International Standard Industrial Classification (ISIC), revision 3. Note: For VAB countries, gross value added at factor cost is used as the denominator (Izvor: WB WD Indicators, 5.8.212.)

Col. 7: Services, etc., value added (% of GDP) - Services correspond to ISIC divisions 50-99 and they include value added in wholesale and retail trade (including hotels and restaurants), transport, and government, financial, professional, and personal services such as education, health care, and real estate services. Also included are imputed bank service charges, import duties, and any statistical discrepancies noted by national compilers as well as discrepancies arising from rescaling. Value added is the net output of a sector after adding up all outputs and subtracting intermediate inputs. It is calculated without making deductions for depreciation of fabricated assets or depletion and degradation of natural resources. The industrial origin of value added is determined by the International Standard Industrial Classification (ISIC), revision 3. Note: For VAB countries, gross value added at factor cost is used as the denominator. (Izvor: WB WD Indicators, 5.8.212.)

Kol. 8: Household final consumption expenditure, etc. (% of GDP) - Household final consumption expenditure (formerly private consumption) is the market value of all goods and services, including durable products (such as cars, washing machines, and home computers), purchased by households. It excludes purchases of dwellings but includes imputed rent for owner-occupied dwellings. It also includes payments and fees to governments to obtain permits and licenses. Here, household consumption expenditure includes the expenditures of nonprofit institutions serving households, even when reported separately by the country. This item also includes any statistical discrepancy in the use of resources relative to the supply of resources. (Izvor: WB WD Indicators, 5.8.212.)

Col. 9: General government final consumption expenditure (% of GDP) -General government final consumption expenditure (formerly general government consumption) includes all government current expenditures for purchases of goods and services (including compensation of employees). It also includes most expenditures on national defense and security, but excludes government military expenditures that are part of government capital formation. (Izvor: WB WD Indicators, 5.8.212.)

Col. 10: Gross capital formation (% of GDP) - Gross capital formation (formerly gross domestic investment) consists of outlays on additions to the fixed assets of the economy plus net changes in the level of inventories. Fixed assets include land improvements (fences, ditches, drains, and so on); plant, machinery, and equipment purchases; and the construction of roads, railways, and the like, including schools, offices, hospitals, private residential dwellings, and commercial and industrial buildings. Inventories are stocks of goods held by firms to meet temporary or unexpected fluctuations in production or sales, and "work in progress." According to the 1993 SNA, net acquisitions of valuables are also considered capital formation. (Izvor: WB WD Indicators, 27.7.2012)

Col. 11: Gross domestic savings (% of GDP) - Gross domestic savings are calculated as GDP less final consumption expenditure (total consumption). (Izvor: WB WD Indicators, 27.7.2012)

Col. 12: External debt stocks, (DOD, per capita mlrd US$) u 2010 - Total external debt is debt owed to nonresidents repayable in foreign currency, goods, or services. It is the sum of public, publicly guaranteed, and private nonguaranteed long-term debt, short-term debt, and use of IMF credit. Data are in current U.S. dollars. - Osnovni izvor: WB WD Indicators, 25. July 2012.; Dopunski: Budući da u WB WD Indicators nisu sadržani podaci o External debt stocks, total (DOD, current US$) za najrazvijenije zemlje, morao je za to biti korišten alternativni izvor - From Wikipedia, List of countries by external debt, last modifed on 24 July 2012